NOTORIOUS AMERICANS AND THEIR TIMES

Joseph

MCCARTHY

and the Cold War

by

VICTORIA SHERROW

BLACKBIRCH PRESS, INC.

WOODBRIDGE, CONNECTICUT

Published by Blackbirch Press, Inc.
260 Amity Road
Woodbridge, CT 06525

e-mail: staff@blackbirch.com
Web site: www.blackbirch.com

©1999 by Blackbirch Press, Inc.
First Edition

Acknowledgment

The publisher would like to thank David M. Oshinsky for his expert review of this work. Professor Oshinsky is the author of *A Conspiracy So Immense: The World of Joe McCarthy*, and a member of the history department at Rutgers University.

Printed in the United States

10 9 8 7 6 5 4 3 2 1

Library of Congress Cataloging-in-Publication Data
Sherrow, Victoria.
Joseph McCarthy and the Cold War / by Victoria Sherrow. — 1st ed.
    p.   cm. — (Notorious Americans and their times)
    Includes bibliographical references and index.
    Summary: A biography of the unknown first-term senator from Wisconsin who gained notoriety by stirring up anti-Communist fears in the years after World War II.
    ISBN 1-56711-219-6 (lib. bdg. : alk. paper)
    1. McCarthy, Joseph, 1908–1957—Juvenile literature. 2. Anti-communist movements—United States—History—20th century—Juvenile literature. 3. Legislators—United States—Biography—Juvenile literature. 4. United States—Congress—Senate—Biography—Juvenile literature. 5. Cold War—Juvenile literature. [1. McCarthy, Joseph, 1908–1957. 2. Legislators. 3. Anti-communist movements—History.]
I. Title. II. Series.
E748.M143S54   1999
973.921'092—dc21   98-15559
[B]   CIP
                                          AC

Table of Contents

Chapter 1

EARLY "RED SCARES"

A YOUNG WISCONSIN LAWYER

*I*n March 1951, film star Larry Parks was questioned by a congressional committee investigating Communist activity in America. "Have you ever been a member of the Communist party?" they asked. Parks admitted that he joined in 1941 because it was the most liberal party he could find. He quit in 1945 from lack of interest. The committee chairman, John S. Wood, then asked Parks to name people who had attended party meetings. Parks refused. "I would prefer," he said, "if you would allow me, not to mention other people's names.... This is not the American way. To force a man to do this is not American justice." The committee threatened to hold him in contempt. They would take legal action against Parks unless he cooperated. Parks replied, "Don't present me with the choice of either being in contempt of this committee and going to jail or forcing me to really crawl through the mud to be an informer."

Opposite: *Joseph McCarthy was one of America's most powerful senators in the early 1950s.*

Politics of Fear

At one time, scenes like this occurred regularly in America. The interrogators were members of Congress; the people being questioned were U.S. citizens. During the 1940s and 1950s, thousands of Americans were falsely accused of having some association with the Communist party. They were forced to swear allegiance to the government or lose their jobs. Investigations were conducted without those legal safeguards we call "due process of law." The accused were assumed to be guilty until proven innocent, instead of the reverse.

The man who played a central role in generating this anti-Communist hysteria was Joseph R. McCarthy, the U.S. senator from Wisconsin. This complex individual has become the symbol of a troubling period in American history that now bears his name—the McCarthy Era.

Principles of Freedom

The men who established the government of the United States declared that people must be free to express their ideas and opinions, even if those ideas are unpopular. They believed people have a right to free expression as long as they respect the rights of others. The right to freedom of speech as well as freedom of religion, the press, and peaceful assembly are set forth in the First Amendment to the Constitution. It says:

> *Congress shall make no law respecting an establishment of religion or prohibiting the free exercise thereof; or abridging the freedom of speech, or of the press; or of the right of the people peaceably to assemble, or to petition the government for a redress of grievances.*

The First Amendment is one of ten amendments that together form the Bill of Rights. In writing them, the framers of the Constitution aimed to protect the rights of all of the nation's citizens.

The First Amendment is sometimes referred to as the "Free Speech Amendment." Over the past 200 years, numerous court cases have been argued on this point, as Americans have continued to interpret the First Amendment and apply it to everyday life. As the world changes, however, new issues concerning free speech arise.

A Tense Post-War World

Change brings stress and uncertainty, and the years after World War II brought changes in many areas of life. There were major discoveries in science and technology. New discoveries brought ways to improve life, but also to destroy it. Advances in electronics led to the invention of computers, which have become more powerful with every passing decade. America launched the

This mushroom cloud followed an atomic blast in the Pacific islands of Micronesia in 1947.

atomic age by exploding the first nuclear bombs. The sobering realization of their destructive capability permanently altered relations between the world's nations.

The political boundaries of the world also changed. In Eastern Europe, the Soviet Union led a powerful bloc (group) of Communist countries. The United States emerged as the leader of the western European nations, most of which were democracies.

As the United States and the nations of Europe squared off into these two alliances, a Cold War replaced the hot conflicts of World War II. Relations between West and East were strained, and sometimes openly hostile. In the United States, the highly publicized trials of people charged with spying for Russia only heightened tension and fear in America. Communism struck fear in many people who believed that such a system of government threatened the American way of life. The right to own property and businesses were basic rights in the United States. In Communist countries, all property and businesses were owned by a strong central government, and the profits were used for the good of the nation. Communist nations had nothing like a Bill of Rights to protect individual liberties.

Worries about Communists were not new in the United States. They dated back to the Russian Revolution of 1917, when a Bolshevik (Communist) victory aroused concerns that such uprisings could occur elsewhere. In the years that followed, Congressional committees investigated activities that they feared might be "subversive"—activities that seemed to promote communism and might lead to the overthrow of the U.S. government. They passed laws banning Communists from holding certain jobs.

Along with others, Senator Joseph McCarthy made use of this fearful atmosphere for his own political purposes. For four years, he warned Americans that a vast Communist conspiracy

Russian soldiers fire rifles in the courtyard of the czar's Winter Palace in St. Petersburg during the Russian Revolution in 1917.

intended to destroy the country. McCarthy portrayed himself as a hero, working to root out traitors. He eventually left the Senate in disgrace, however, as a result of his ruthless tactics.

Today, historians consider the McCarthy years a modern-day witch-hunt that destroyed people's lives. The word "McCarthyism" has come to stand for the use of false charges and other unethical tactics to limit someone's free speech.

A Wisconsin Boyhood

Joseph Raymond McCarthy was the fourth of seven children born to a Wisconsin farm family. Records from Grand Chute Township show he was born on November 14, 1908, though McCarthy sometimes said he was born later in order to take a year or two off of his age.

Few details are known about McCarthy's childhood, and he told people little about his early years. His grandfather, Stephen McCarthy, came to the United States from Ireland in the 1840s. For ten years, he worked in upstate New York, saving enough money to buy land in Wisconsin in 1859. Three years later, he married Margaret Stoffel, and together they had ten children.

Over the years, Stephen McCarthy bought more land so that his children could live nearby. Timothy, Joseph McCarthy's father, rented some of this land. He and his Irish-born wife, Bridget Tierney, raised their own large family in Grand Chute. Their lives revolved around family, hard work, and their Catholic faith. Although the soil was poor, the McCarthys managed to make a living. Their hard work and thrifty ways enabled them to move from a log cabin into a house shortly before Joseph was born. Like other families in their Irish-American neighborhood, the McCarthys had no indoor plumbing or electricity.

Joseph remained close to his family throughout his life. Some of his biographers describe an awkward and shy boy who was teased by his peers. But in conversations with the historian David M. Oshinsky, McCarthy's childhood friends and neighbors described a different sort of boy. "They remember him as a vigorous, extroverted, ruggedly handsome boy," Oshinsky said. These people recalled that Joe obeyed his parents and was helpful and energetic. He never seemed to sit still for very long. He worked hard on the farm and held other part-time jobs, which enabled him to contribute to the family's income.

The McCarthys did not have much money, and neither did their neighbors. Childhood poverty and a desire to prove himself may have shaped McCarthy's strong ambitions as an adult. As a senator, he sometimes criticized people who were born rich and enjoyed fine homes and other advantages they had never worked for.

McCarthy's formal education began in the Underhill Country School, where his teacher taught eight grades in a single room. McCarthy was known for his strong memory and his ability to learn quickly.

"Red Scares"

During McCarthy's youth, major changes were occurring around the world. In 1917, the Russian Revolution toppled more than two centuries of harsh rule by the country's powerful czars. The new Bolshevik leaders introduced laws that were equally strict, and they ordered the murder of Czar Nicholas and his family.

Newspapers and Russian refugees described the Bolshevik (later called Communist) takeover and the bloody civil war that followed. The Communists seized private property and took control of almost every aspect of Russian life: the economy, educational system, international trade, and the arts. They also disbanded religious institutions in Russia. (When a number of republics along its borders were combined with Russia in 1922, the new nation was called the Union of Soviet Socialist Republics, or the Soviet Union.) The Communists censored what people could say, teach, and write. Condemning the government was illegal.

To many Americans, the word "communism" meant the death of free speech and religion, and the imposition of harsh governmental control. They feared that the Russians planned to dominate the world, and that American Communists would help by overthrowing the U.S. government from within its own borders.

By the time Joseph McCarthy was an adolescent, America had already experienced its first "Red Scares." A "Red Scare" was a period in U.S. history when many citizens were especially fearful of Communists. (The color red was used as a Communist symbol.)

One night in June 1919, a bomb exploded at the front door of A. Mitchell Palmer, the newly appointed U.S. attorney general. Palmer was unhurt, although the bomber himself died in the blast. Bombs exploded that night at the homes of other high-ranking government officials in eight American cities. Most people blamed the explosions on the Communists.

In response to the bombings, Congress set up the Anti-Radical Division to investigate and prosecute people who were viewed as a threat to the government. Twenty-four-year-old John "J." Edgar Hoover was chosen to head the division.

J. Edgar Hoover headed the Anti-Radical Division before he became director of the Federal Bureau of Investigation from 1924 to 1972.

In 1919 and 1920, hundreds of Russian immigrants who were not yet U.S. citizens were deported for political reasons. Some of them had not taken part in any Communist activities. Others belonged to Communist groups but had not acted in any way against the government.

During the next few years, thousands of people were arrested for belonging to Communist groups, including U.S. citizens. And more organizations and activities were labeled "Communist" by worried Americans. Labor leaders and union members aroused suspicion. In 1919, when workers went on strike in Seattle, Washington, opponents called them "Communists." The mayor said the strike leaders aimed to "take possession of our American Government and try to duplicate the anarchy [absence of law] in Russia."

The first Red Scare quieted down in the early 1920s. Americans' fears of communism would rise and fall in the years that followed, reaching its most dangerous peak during the 1950s.

Work and Then School

In 1922, at age 14, McCarthy decided to work full-time instead of going to school. He rented land from his father to raise chickens, increasing his flock from 50 to 10,000 birds within just a few years. His farm was thriving when McCarthy caught pneumonia in 1927. While he was sick, McCarthy's hired workers neglected the chickens, and disease wiped out his flocks.

After he recovered, McCarthy moved to nearby Manawa, Wisconsin, where he ran a grocery store. He drew many new customers by expanding the store's hours and advertising its products. His hard work and intelligence impressed townspeople. Mrs. Frank Osterlith, who owned the home where McCarthy boarded, urged him to return to school. Although McCarthy was then nearly 20 years old, he decided to go to Little Wolf High School.

With personal help from the principal, Leo Hershberger, McCarthy completed high school in just one year. He rose before dawn each day to study, attended school for nine hours, and spent evenings working at a movie theater. At his graduation ceremony, McCarthy was singled out for special praise. Hershberger said, "We have never graduated a student more capable of graduating."

College Years

In 1930, McCarthy enrolled as an engineering student at Marquette University in Milwaukee, Wisconsin. The Great Depression had begun in 1929. It was a period when businesses failed and workers lost their jobs. Those who still had jobs saw their wages shrink. Like most other students, McCarthy worked many hours a week to pay for his education. He found time, though, to join the debating and the varsity boxing teams. After he won his first boxing match, a newspaper noted enthusiastically that "his pile-driving lefts and rights...battered Al Razor to the canvas three times in the first round and allowed him to coast to victory."

McCarthy's inconsistent behavior surprised his friends. He loved to play poker, and he sometimes drank too much. After a night of card games and heavy drinking, however, he would put on a suit and attend church.

By 1931, McCarthy decided to become a lawyer. He thought he could make better use of his strong memory and outgoing personality than he would as an engineer. To study law, he would need additional schooling at Marquette University. Because the Depression was becoming worse, he also had to spend many hours working odd jobs.

America During the Great Depression

Throughout the nation, the poverty created by the Great Depression was stunning. Long lines of hungry people formed at soup kitchens, where they waited for free meals. Many Americans suffered from poor nutrition. Local governments did not have enough resources to provide food, shelter, clothing, and health care to the increasing numbers of people who needed them.

During the Depression, some Americans lived in poverty in small villages of shacks. The villages were called "Hoovervilles," after President Herbert Hoover.

The Depression made people rethink their political beliefs. Some Americans, especially young people and intellectuals, examined different systems of government. They joined political groups or attended meetings and lectures to learn more about socialism and communism, two very similar political systems. They wondered whether one of these systems could solve the nation's economic problems.

Those already committed to communism demanded change. They argued that the nation's wealth should be distributed more equally among Americans. And they called for more rights for workers.

Democrats and Republicans expressed a variety of opinions about what the role of the government should be. They ranged from liberals, who thought the government should take more control of the economy, to conservatives, who wanted the government to interfere as little as possible. Regardless of their beliefs, Americans took it for granted that they could express their ideas and attend any meetings they chose. Years later, however, they were called to account for their activities during this period.

A Young Lawyer

In 1935, Joseph McCarthy received his law degree from Marquette. He had served as class president and coached the boxing team in addition to working to support himself.

The Depression was still casting its shadow on the nation when McCarthy opened a law office in Waupaca, in eastern Wisconsin. During the year that he practiced there, he handled few cases. His colleagues viewed him as a disorganized man who earned more money playing poker than he did as an attorney. Some thought that McCarthy was insensitive to the standards and values of the community. One man commented, "I've always felt that Joe lived in a different moral universe. He asked himself only two questions: 'What do I want and how do I get it.' Once he got rolling, you had to step aside."

In 1936, McCarthy left Waupaca to join a law practice in nearby Shawano. He became active in politics, hoping to get elected to a political office. As president of the Young Democrats Club in his district, McCarthy campaigned for President Franklin D. Roosevelt's re-election, praising the president's New Deal programs. That same year, he ran for district attorney and lost. Then McCarthy returned to his law firm.

Discouraging "Subversives"

During the late 1930s, the U.S. government took steps to discourage Communist activity. In 1938, Congress passed the Hatch Act, which stated that Communist party members could not hold federal jobs.

That same year, Congress formed the House Committee on Un-American Activities (called HUAC). Its chairman, Martin Dies, had suggested that a congressional committee investigate "subversion."

During the early years, HUAC followed a policy of "guilt by association." People were called in for questioning if they had joined left-wing political groups that had Communists among their members. People summoned by the committee often lost the trust of their employers and then their jobs.

Some people came before the committee voluntarily to attack their enemies. In August 1938, John P. Frey, the president of the metal workers division of the American Federation of Labor (AFL), testified that a rival union, the Congress of Industrial Organizations (CIO) was under Communist control.

During the 1930s, President Roosevelt introduced government programs that were meant to aid the victims of the Depression. These relief programs became known as the "New Deal." The New Deal was not popular with Republicans and conservative Democrats. They fought the Social Security Act of 1935, which provided retirement money for older citizens as well as unemployment insurance for adults of all ages. Roosevelt's opponents also objected to the Works Project Administration (WPA) programs that were established to provide employment. They claimed the government was interfering with private businesses.

HUAC's chairman, J. Parnell Thomas, especially disliked a WPA program called the Federal Theater Project. It produced thousands of plays in communities throughout the nation. Along with Shakespearean dramas and other classics, the group performed plays about current events. Some of these productions featured African Americans and other minorities. The director of the WPA, Hallie Flanagan, felt the plays should reflect a "consciousness of the art and economics" of the times.

J. Parnell Thomas said that the theater promoted ideas that were too liberal. He and his supporters convinced Congress not to fund this program after 1938.

Roosevelt's New Deal programs were not popular with conservatives. Here the president is shown greeting farmers.

He gave HUAC a list of 283 people and local CIO unions that he said were Communist. Although Frey gave no proof to back up his charges, some people accepted them as fact.

The people on Frey's list suffered serious consequences. They were not allowed to appear before HUAC to defend themselves. But they were fired from their jobs, and other companies would not hire them.

Some members of Congress criticized HUAC's tactics. Congressman Maury Maverick said HUAC had broad powers "to investigate, humiliate, meddle with anything and everything." The U.S. Supreme Court declared that HUAC's procedures violated people's rights. Nevertheless, HUAC continued to do its work.

Concerns over communism and subversive activity persisted. In 1940, the Alien Registration Act (known as the "Smith Act") made it illegal to belong to a group that supported a violent overthrow of the U.S. government. By 1941, some federal agencies were investigating the loyalty of their employees.

Dramatic world events overshadowed these concerns for several years, however. In 1939, World War II erupted in Europe, as Nazi Germany occupied one nation after another. A continent away, Japan attacked countries in Asia and the South Pacific. The United States would soon enter the war, and—ironically—one of its allies would be the Communist-controlled Soviet Union.

Chapter 2

THE POST-WAR YEARS
"TAIL-GUNNER JOE" IN THE SENATE

By 1939, McCarthy had abandoned his Democratic roots to become a Republican. He was ready to run for office again, this time for circuit judge in the Tenth Judicial District. (Circuit court judges preside over cases arising in the counties or districts that make up their region.)

McCarthy's political ambitions led to a falling-out with his law partner, who had also planned to run for judge. When McCarthy entered the race, his partner asked him to leave the firm.

McCarthy was determined to win, and he spent as much as 20 hours a day making speeches and visiting people to chat with them about their problems. The husky, thick-browed candidate became a familiar figure in the district. During the campaign, McCarthy attacked his opponent, Judge Edgar Werner, who had been the circuit judge for 24 years. Werner was 66 years old, but McCarthy repeatedly called him "my 73-year-old opponent." He also lowered his own age, from almost 31 to 29. (By doing so, McCarthy made himself out to be the youngest circuit judge in state history.) His tactics seemed to contradict his campaign motto, "Justice Is Truth in Action."

McCarthy won a surprise victory and was instantly regarded as an up-and-coming politician. The new judge had his critics, however. Some of them accused him of using illegal campaign tactics. They charged that McCarthy had spent more money than state election laws allowed and that he had lied about Judge Werner's age. It was the first of many times that McCarthy's political methods would be challenged.

Judge McCarthy was praised for working hard, but he was also known for ignoring proper legal procedures when they were inconvenient. For example, in order to dispense with a divorce case quickly, McCarthy granted the divorce while walking into the courthouse with the two people involved. An article in the *Milwaukee Journal* offered some blunt criticism:

> *Judge McCarthy, whose burning ambition for political advancement is accompanied by an astonishing disregard for things ethical and traditional, is doing serious injury to the judiciary in this state.*

Wartime Service

On December 7, 1941, Japanese war planes bombed the U.S. naval base at Pearl Harbor, Hawaii, prompting the United States to enter World War II. America fought with the Soviet Union and several other nations against the Axis powers of Germany, Italy, and Japan.

An American ship burns after the Japanese attack in Pearl Harbor on December 7, 1941.

McCarthy joined the U.S. Marines Corps at the age of 33. He was leaving a vacancy on the circuit court, but he refused to resign from his judicial office. As a result, other judges had to handle McCarthy's work along with their own.

Commissioned as a first lieutenant, McCarthy remained in the corps from June 1942 through December 1944. In 1944, he decided to run for the U.S. Senate. He campaigned for the nomination in July during his 32-day leave. McCarthy didn't seem troubled by a Wisconsin law that banned sitting judges from running for office. A military ruling also forbade officers from speaking out on political issues. McCarthy got around the military law by making speeches in which he expressed regret that he could not speak about various issues, such as national defense. He added that if he *could* speak, this is what he'd say.... Then he went on to give his opinions. McCarthy lost the election, but two years later, in 1946, he was ready to make a second run for the U.S. Senate.

McCarthy Deceives the Voters

Before enlisting in the marines, McCarthy had confided to friends that a war record was essential for his political future. During his second senatorial campaign, he distributed campaign literature that falsified his military record. In the literature, he was described as a combat veteran, when in fact McCarthy held a desk job as an intelligence officer, someone who gathered information about the enemy. He had gone along as an observer on some military flights that held little danger, and he made sure to have himself photographed. Then he distributed photos of himself riding in the tail-gun (rear) position of a dive bomber, and called himself

McCarthy poses in a dive bomber. He used photographs such as this one to create the false impression that he was in combat during World War II.

"Tail-Gunner Joe." His catchy campaign slogan was "Congress Needs a Tail-Gunner." McCarthy also led people to think he received a leg wound during combat, when he actually fell from the ladder of a ship and broke his foot during an on-board party.

Wisconsin voters were either unaware of these falsehoods or ignored them. McCarthy won the 1946 election and joined the U.S. Senate as America moved into the post–World War II period. For the first time in ten years, the Senate had a Republican majority.

During the campaign, some Republican candidates had engaged in "red-baiting" (accusing others of being Communists). For example, a Republican leader in Illinois, Robert McCormick, said, "Everyone knows that the Democratic Party is the party of the Russian-loving Communists in this country." A new and more intense wave of Red Scares was beginning.

A "Cold War"

The end of World War II on September 2, 1945, set the stage for a tense political climate. Before the war, America had an uneasy relationship with the Soviet Union, and many people distrusted its leader, Joseph Stalin. However, the two countries united successfully against Hitler. Americans were impressed by the fact that Soviet troops fought hard and suffered many casualties. The Soviet Union played a key role in Germany's defeat.

In February 1945, President Roosevelt, English Prime Minister Winston Churchill, and Joseph Stalin had met in Yalta, a Soviet resort area on the Black Sea. They gathered to discuss the division of the lands that were liberated from the Axis powers. The Yalta agreement stated that Germany would be divided into four occupation zones: American, British, French, and Soviet. Part of eastern Poland would go to the Soviet Union, along with

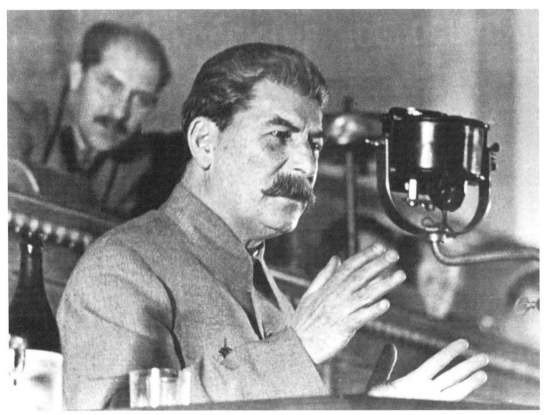

Joseph Stalin, leader of the Soviet Union from 1924 to 1953, invaded the nations of Eastern Europe after World War II.

some territory in the north and west that had been occupied by Germany. The agreement also stated that free elections would be held in Poland after the war, and that eventually, all of the liberated European nations would have free elections. Two months after the meeting in Yalta, President Roosevelt died suddenly. Harry S. Truman became the nation's new president.

The former allies soon became enemies. Stalin sent troops into Eastern Europe and installed Communist governments in Poland, Yugoslavia, Hungary, Rumania, Bulgaria, Albania, and eventually, in Czechoslovakia. This group of nations became known as the

Soviet, or Eastern, Bloc. Western leaders were outraged by Stalin's decision to ignore the Allies' wartime agreements.

Relations worsened after the Soviet Union developed nuclear weapons. During the war, the United States had conducted a top-secret effort to build atomic weapons, which were made from energy produced by either splitting or fusing atoms. The program was called the "Manhattan Project." President Roosevelt authorized the project after he was informed that German scientists were working to create their own atomic bombs. Germany failed to develop them, but the United States released two atomic bombs on Japan in response to Japan's (non-atomic) bombing of Pearl Harbor.

A British scientist named Klaus Fuchs was one of many scientists who worked on the Manhattan Project. It was later discovered that Fuchs had provided Soviet scientists with information that helped them in their own atomic research.

When the Soviets began testing atomic (also called "nuclear") weapons in 1949, many Americans were stunned that their enemies had this military capability. An arms race followed between the United States and the Soviet Union. Each side wanted to have newer and more destructive weapons than its opponent, and in greater quantities.

Truman Takes Action

Even before the Soviet Union tested its nuclear weapons, and well before Fuchs's espionage was revealed, President Truman received many reports that Communist spies were working in the U.S. government and providing the Soviets with secret information.

In response, Truman issued Executive Order 9835, which permitted a large-scale investigation to determine whether or not federal employees were loyal to the U.S. government. This investigation lasted four years and cleared more than 3 million employees of any suspicious behavior. Only 212 people were dismissed because their loyalty was questioned, and no outright spies were uncovered. Truman decided that in the future, any employees involved in sensitive (secret) work who were suspected of subversion could be dismissed.

In March 1947, the president announced the Truman Doctrine, a policy for the containment of communism overseas. Truman vowed that the United States would help the "free peoples who are resisting attempted subjugation [oppression] by armed minorities or by outside pressures." He established the right of the United States

During the 1940s, President Harry Truman adopted a number of measures to fight communism at home and abroad.

to interfere in the politics of other nations in order to prevent communism from spreading.

Truman also approved the revival of the Smith Act of 1940, which had been set aside during World War II. (See page 19.) Under the act, twelve leaders of the American Communist party were charged with engaging in subversive activities in 1949. All except the national party chairman, William Foster, who was ill and did not stand trial, were found guilty and sent to prison.

In October 1947, HUAC opened hearings in Washington, D.C., to explore subversion in the film industry. Among other things, HUAC charged that many motion pictures contained "Communist propaganda." Between 1945 and 1957, HUAC held about 230 public hearings and required more than 3,000 people to testify.

Some actors and actresses became witnesses, voluntarily giving information to the committee. But one group of ten producers, directors, and screenwriters strongly opposed HUAC. They were supporters of Joseph Stalin, and they became known as the "Hollywood Ten." Writer John Howard Lawson was among them. When he testified on October 27, 1947, he asked to read a statement that he had prepared:

For a week, this committee has conducted an illegal and indecent trial of American citizens....

I am plastered with mud because I happen to be an American who expresses opinions that the House Un-American Activities Committee does not like.... The issue is my right to have opinions....

The HUAC chairman would not allow Lawson to read this statement, which Lawson then released to the press.

The Hollywood Ten continued to protest being called before HUAC and refused to answer questions, calling the entire process unconstitutional. They were cited for "contempt of court."

Some people who disliked the political views of the Hollywood Ten nevertheless agreed in principle with their stand against HUAC. In 1947, sympathizers from the film industry organized a combined delegation of 50 directors, writers, and actors, among them the actors Humphrey Bogart, Ronald Reagan, Groucho Marx, and John Huston. The group flew from California to Washington, D.C., to challenge the investigative tactics of HUAC and support the civil rights of the accused. During stops in Kansas City, St. Louis, and Chicago, they discussed their mission with the press.

The Hollywood Ten remained uncooperative and they eventually served some time in jail. Fearing HUAC, film producers agreed not to hire any of the Hollywood Ten unless they declared under oath that they were no longer Communists.

An Undistinguished Senator

During the late 1940s, McCarthy was settling into his first term in Washington. The new senator from Wisconsin did not make a strong impression, and his party gave him a small role on an unimportant committee.

The Hollywood Ten and their two lawyers arrive at a U.S. district courthouse.

For the next ten years, the "Ten" and many others could not work openly. Some screenwriters used pseudonyms (false names) and worked for less pay. In addition, producers spread the word that people in the film industry who were suspected of being Communists would be informally "blacklisted," and would therefore be ineligible for employment anywhere in the industry.

For three years, McCarthy's senatorial career was fairly uneventful, though he did get himself into trouble because of a business connection. In 1948, McCarthy received $10,000 from the Lustron Corporation, a company that made prefabricated houses. (They were partially assembled at the factory.) Lustron said this money was payment for a 7,000-word pamphlet urging the government to give financial support for prefabricated houses. McCarthy was listed as the author. Earlier, McCarthy had opposed bills to fund government housing that would compete with Lustron's products. It seemed that the Lustron Company was improperly influencing Senator McCarthy's voting.

To further complicate matters, McCarthy was a member of the Banking and Currency Committee. The committee oversaw federal housing agencies, including the Reconstruction Finance Corporation (RFC). At the time Lustron paid McCarthy $10,000, the company was being investigated by the RFC because Lustron owed the RFC $37 million and had never repaid that debt.

McCarthy was criticized for his conduct. In 1949, after the Democrats regained a majority in the Senate, a new chairman was selected for the Banking and Currency Committee. He called McCarthy a troublemaker and said he would not be part of the committee unless McCarthy left. The Republicans cooperated and reassigned McCarthy to the Committee on the District of Columbia, widely regarded as the least important assignment in the Senate.

Those who knew McCarthy during this period described him as ambitious but unsure of how to make his mark. He was a loyal Republican, but he didn't contribute to important policy-making decisions. Some noticed that he was a careless dresser.

McCarthy changed his image by wearing more appealing ties and neat, dark suits. He appeared at more social events, and some hostesses even considered him an attractive bachelor.

Relief for War-Torn Europe

During McCarthy's first term, Congress considered legislation involving U.S. aid to countries that were still suffering econom-ically as a result of World War II. The most ambitious proposal was the Marshall Plan, designed by the former army general George C. Marshall. He had served as Roosevelt's chief military advisor during the war, and then became Truman's secretary of state.

The United States pledged to help European countries rebuild their public works—such as roads and schools—as well as their factories. The plan would provide jobs for millions of Europeans. Sixteen European nations and West Germany agreed to participate. Congress set aside more than $5 billion for the plan, which Marshall called "a mighty offensive *against* hunger, poverty, desperation, and chaos" that would promote a world "in which free institutions can exist."

McCarthy opposed the Marshall Plan. He did not like Truman's Point Four program, either. It offered technical assistance and military aid to non-Communist countries in Asia, Africa, Central America, and South America. His opposition was puzzling, since both programs aimed to encourage democracy abroad. Countries receiving aid would learn about the economic and social benefits of the American form of government.

Rising Concerns

Communism became an issue in the 1948 presidential election. That year, the Soviets refused to settle the status of Berlin, a German city that had been divided into four zones, just like the rest of country. The Soviets demanded that their currency be used in all four of the city's zones—Soviet, American, British, and French. Then in June, the Soviets announced a blockade that would bar traffic on roads, railroads, and canals entering the Soviet zone, in East Berlin. The blockade made it impossible for the Allies to enter or leave West Berlin over existing land routes. In response, the United States organized an airlift and flew in food, fuel, medicine, clothing, and other supplies needed by the more than 2 million people living in the three Allied zones. During these tense months, Truman feared the Soviets would attack Allied planes, which had to cross Soviet air space in Berlin. But the Soviet Union avoided a confrontation and ended the blockade in May 1949.

By that time, a Communist revolution in China that had been going on for decades reached a crisis point. The Nationalist government of Chiang Kai-shek had failed to provide the economic and social reforms that many Chinese wanted. Communists led by Mao Zedong received an increasing amount of popular support,

Fuel and food was air-lifted into the Allied zones of Berlin during the Soviet blockade of 1948 and 1949.

The Alger Hiss Case

Political tensions were running high when a scandal erupted in July 1948. Whittaker Chambers, an editor for *Time* magazine and a former Communist, testified before HUAC about his espionage (spying) activities. He claimed that two spy rings were operating for the Soviets in Washington, D.C. Chambers named Alger Hiss, a former high-ranking official in the State Department, as one of his spying partners. Hiss, age 42, had held important government posts during the Roosevelt Administration. In 1947, he became president of an organization called the Carnegie Endowment for International Peace.

When Chambers made his accusations public, Hiss sued him for libel (for ruining his reputation). In response, Chambers produced documents that he said supported his

claims. Hiss replied that they were forgeries. During a congressional investigation, a California congressman and future president named Richard Nixon played a prominent role in attacking Hiss.

Alger Hiss

Hiss was convicted only of perjury—lying under oath—because too much time had passed since he was first accused of espionage. But most scholars now agree that he was probably a spy.

and they also had military equipment sent by the Soviets. The United States had been sending troops and supplies to Chiang Kai-shek, but the U.S. Army withdrew its troops in 1947. U.S. military leaders told President Truman that the Nationalists needed far more long-term assistance than America could reasonably supply.

In December 1949, Chiang Kai-shek fled the mainland with 2 million of his followers and established a state on the island of Formosa (now called Taiwan). The new island nation, called Nationalist China, had a population of about 10 million. Mao Zedong became the chairman (leader) of the mainland country, renamed the People's Republic of China. It was home to 800 million people.

Fearful Americans began calling the People's Republic "Red China." Some believed this vast nation posed an even greater threat than the Soviet Union.

The Cold War Line-up

After the Chinese Revolution, other nations took sides. Some recognized the mainland government as the "real" China, and others chose Taiwan (Nationalist China). The Soviets signed a military treaty with the People's Republic. The United States sided with Taiwan and refused to trade with the People's Republic or keep a U.S. representative there. Many western nations followed the Americans' example.

The United States had strengthened its ties with its western allies through a new treaty signed in April 1949. Based on this agreement, 12 nations in the North Atlantic—the United States, Canada, Great Britain, France, Italy, Belgium, the Netherlands, Luxembourg, Portugal, Denmark, Norway, and Iceland—formed the North Atlantic Treaty Organization (NATO) in 1950. Greece and Turkey joined NATO in 1952, and West Germany was admitted in 1955.

NATO nations pledged to aid any member who was attacked by a foreign power, using military force if necessary. The treaty also declared that NATO nations would cooperate for military and economic purposes during peacetime. NATO headquarters were established in Paris, and General Dwight D. Eisenhower was named the head of the organization.

The post-war world contained two blocs, a western one and an eastern one, led by two nations regarded as "superpowers"— the United States and the Soviet Union. For several decades to come, they would view each other with mutual distrust. As the fifties began, tough talk by the Soviets, and the spread of communism, inspired fear and even panic in the United States.

For Americans, this would be a decade of hula hoops, rock and roll, fast-food hamburgers, and television. Employment was high and the prices of consumer goods were fairly low. Many Americans bought homes for the first time and enjoyed using dishwashers, vacuum cleaners, and other time-saving appliances. More people than ever before made economic strides as the result of the "G.I. Bill," which offered free higher education to war veterans. But lurking beneath the era's optimism and relative prosperity was the knowledge that two powerful enemy nations each had weapons that could blow up the world.

Chapter 3

HUNTING COMMUNISTS
McCARTHY FINDS THE RIGHT ISSUE

McCarthy was up for re-election in 1952. As 1950 approached, he realized he had little support. Contributions to his campaign were weak, and his opponents seemed confident they could win his seat.

The *Milwaukee Journal*, a frequent critic, and the *Capital Times* were among the Wisconsin newspapers that attacked him. They described McCarthy's dismal record in the Senate and reported that he had not declared all of his income on his tax returns. (The Department of Taxation later required him to pay $2,677.)

Determined to be re-elected, McCarthy needed an issue he could use to his advantage. One January evening, he discussed his problem with some friends, including the Reverend Edmund

Walsh, dean of the Georgetown University School of Foreign Service. Father Walsh broached the subject of communism.

It was hardly a new issue. Magazines and newspapers discussed communism regularly. In March 1947, for example, *Look* magazine published an article called "How to Spot a Communist." The author of the article warned, "Check before you sign that petition or join that little-known club; you might be supporting a secret club."

McCarthy had not seemed very interested in communism before, but now he showed great interest and told his companions enthusiastically, "That's it. The government is full of Communists. We can hammer away at them." The senator had found his "hot-button" issue and soon had a chance to test it out.

Startling Allegations

In February 1950, McCarthy was scheduled to speak at three fund-raising events, which were a Republican tradition on Lincoln's Birthday. McCarthy decided to discuss Communist subversion. Before leaving Washington, he asked Willard Edwards, a reporter for *The Chicago Tribune*, to help him draft a speech. Edwards had written articles on this subject for his paper, which was known for its right-wing political philosophy.

At his first talk, in Wheeling, West Virginia, McCarthy launched into a history of United States–Soviet relations. He declared that the two nations were "engaged in a showdown fight" that pitted "our Western Christian world" against the "Communist world," which did not believe in God. According to McCarthy, America was losing the battle and growing weaker in relation to its opponent. He said the threat to the nation was coming from within, from Americans who were traitors. McCarthy declared these traitors were:

...those who have been treated so well by this nation...who have had all the benefits that the wealthiest nation on earth has had to offer—the finest homes, the finest college educations, and the finest jobs in Government we can give. This is glaringly true in the State Department. There the bright young men who are born with silver spoons in their mouths are the ones that have been the worst.

Those who heard the speech later recalled the dramatic moment that followed. McCarthy held up a piece of paper, claiming that on it were written the names of 205 members of the Communist Party who were working in the State Department.

These grave accusations created a furor. The Associated Press agency wrote an account of McCarthy's speech, which appeared in several newspapers. *The Chicago Tribune* and other papers known for their conservative slant gave it the most coverage. McCarthy's words made sense to many Americans. Some of them sought explanations for the spread of communism abroad. Others resented expanding social welfare programs and the rising influence of labor unions at home.

The State Department promptly sent McCarthy a telegram asking for the names of the "Communists" so they could investigate. McCarthy did not reply.

When his plane reached Denver, where he was to give a second speech, reporters asked McCarthy for the 205 names on the list. He told them he had left the list on the plane. He reached Salt Lake City later that day. Again, reporters asked for the list he had mentioned in Wheeling.

No such list existed. (McCarthy would later admit that the paper he had held up was "a laundry list.") He told reporters he had been misquoted and that the 205 people he mentioned were not actually Communists but rather "security (national

McCarthy testifies before a Senate committee in 1951.

safety) risks." This term was broader and could include people who were alcoholics and those with personal problems that exposed them to blackmail.

Now he declared that his list held 57 names of "card-carrying Communists" who worked in the State Department. McCarthy said that if Secretary of State Dean Acheson telephoned him, he would "be glad to give him the names of those 57 card-carrying Communists."

Overnight, it seemed, McCarthy had captured the national spotlight. People praised him for taking a strong public stand against communism, and McCarthy began receiving supportive letters from fans around the country. Many sent checks and cash—dimes, quarters, dollars, and larger amounts—for him to use for his cause. (Evidence later showed that McCarthy deposited the money into his personal bank accounts.)

McCarthy had critics as well as supporters. Some newspapers called his accusations vague. They noted the inconsistencies in his speeches. A *New York Times* columnist compared McCarthy's tactics to "hit-and-run" drivers who leave their victims behind. The Senate ordered him to explain the accusations he had made.

"A Communist Connection"

On February 20, McCarthy walked onto the U.S. Senate floor, carrying a briefcase filled with papers. He proceeded to deliver a six-hour speech about the Communists working in the State Department. His fellow senators tried to sort out the facts about McCarthy's list of Communists. It seemed that he had relied on reports from 1946, when the State Department screened 3,000 employees who had been transferred from other agencies. The department had decided that 285 of those people should not be hired permanently. Seventy-nine had already left when the screening process ended. McCarthy derived the number "205" by incorrectly subtracting 79 from 285, which actually equals 206. Now, four years later, many of the 205 (really 206) people had already left the State Department.

During his long speech, McCarthy claimed he knew of "fifty-seven cases of individuals who would appear to be either card-carrying members or certainly loyal to the Communist party." Senator Scott Lucas of Illinois lost his patience and insisted, "I want him to name those Communists."

McCarthy declined. As the hours passed, he admitted that some people on his list no longer worked at the State Department and some might not be Communists. Prodded by Senator Brian McMahon of Connecticut, McCarthy acknowledged he did not possess complete files on these cases.

Several senators said McCarthy lacked evidence to support his claims. He repeatedly used two tactics: avoidance and attack. He alternately changed topics and threw out new accusations. Or he criticized those who tried to pin him down. At one point, he said that an opponent "thinks this should be a trial of the man digging out the Communists and not of the Communists themselves." He hinted that his critics must be Communist sympathizers. McCarthy refused to identify his sources of information, claiming their jobs would be jeopardized.

When the night finally ended, many senators felt confused and frustrated. Some believed McCarthy had made groundless allegations, but they could not force him to admit it.

Newspapers gave more space to McCarthy's accusations than to examining their accuracy. McCarthy also appeared on television. When the interviewer on the popular news show *Meet the Press* asked why he was crusading against communism, he replied, "It's just one of those tasks that someone has to do." Although he had obviously made use of his anti-Communist crusade for his own political benefit, those closest to him said he sincerely believed in his cause.

McCarthy's "Fraud and a Hoax"

On March 8, 1950, there was a meeting of the Tydings Committee, a Senate subcommittee chaired by Millard E. Tydings of Maryland. The committee members asked McCarthy to prove the charges he had made. Tydings promised "one of the most complete investigations ever given in the history of the Republic."

Linus Pauling was a chemist who worried about the dangers that nuclear weapons posed for mankind. He had won two Nobel Prizes for chemistry, which made him one of the most respected scientists in the world. After World War II, he supported peaceful solutions to world conflicts and international bans on nuclear weapons.

Pauling had been associated with the California Institute of Technology, a state university, since the 1920s. The state of California had actively investigated Communist subversion and required state employees to take oaths of loyalty to the U.S. government. In 1950, the California State Senate Investigating Committee, a state group similar to HUAC, sent Pauling a subpoena (legal summons) to appear. Pauling objected on principle to loyalty oaths. He also declared that U.S. citizens should not be required to explain their political beliefs in public. He expressed these thoughts to the committee.

The committee threatened to prosecute Pauling if he did not answer their questions. Again, Pauling refused, calling their demands a violation of the Constitution. Outside the committee hearing, Pauling told reporters he "was not and never had been" a Communist. "I'm a Rooseveltian Democrat," said the 49-year-old scientist.

Pauling paid a price for his refusal to cooperate. For several years, the government denied him a passport, which meant he could not attend scientific meetings abroad. But his appearances before the committee generated much publicity, which Pauling used to speak out against nuclear weapons and other issues that concerned him.

McCarthy still refused to name his sources. He offended the Tydings Committee members by calling them tools of the State Department. When the committee refused to back off, McCarthy finally named names. The first was Dorothy Kenyon, a former municipal court judge in New York City. Kenyon had never worked for the State Department. Outraged, she called McCarthy "an unmitigated liar."

Kenyon insisted on appearing before the committee to clear her name. At a hearing, she explained that, years ago, she had joined groups that she believed were pursuing worthwhile

Linus Pauling, the Nobel Prize–winning chemist, refused to cooperate with HUAC in 1950.

social reforms. She had resigned from some groups after realizing they had Communist links; the other groups had dissolved years ago. Kenyon called the charges against her "utterly false" and claimed they had "seriously jeopardized, if not destroyed" her good name. She said that she firmly opposed communism.

The committee found no evidence that Kenyon was disloyal. The press agreed, calling her sincere. *Time* magazine called McCarthy "loud-mouthed and irresponsible," however.

McCarthy continued making accusations that cast doubt on people's political loyalties, forcing them to defend themselves.

Nobody he named was proven guilty, however. He gained a lot of attention when he promised to name the top Russian spy in America. He said, "I will stand or fall on this one. If I am shown to be wrong on this, I think the subcommittee would be justified in not taking my other cases too seriously."

He named Owen J. Lattimore, a 49-year-old professor who had served as a political advisor in China during World War II. When Lattimore heard this news, he told reporters for the Associated Press that he was "delighted his whole case rests on me as this means he will fall flat on his face."

The Tydings Committee asked FBI director J. Edgar Hoover to testify regarding secret files on Lattimore. Hoover said he had studied the files and found nothing to support McCarthy's claim.

After four months, the Tydings Committee issued a report on McCarthy's accusations that split along party lines. Democrats, who were the majority, said McCarthy had perpetrated "a fraud and a hoax [trick]" using "half-truths and untruth." The Senate, where Democrats also held a majority, approved the Tydings Committee report. McCarthy soon got even with Millard Tydings.

McCarthy called the report "a signal to the traitors, Communists, and fellow travelers in our Government that they need have no fear of exposure." He continued to make fiery speeches that received plenty of publicity. That year, he campaigned against some of his Democratic enemies in the Senate who were up for re-election, including Senate Majority Leader Scott Lucas of Illinois and Millard Tydings of Maryland. McCarthy accused Tydings of shielding Communists in high places. When Lucas and Tydings lost, some people said it showed McCarthy's power and influence.

While the controversy surrounding McCarthy's list of Communists raged, HUAC continued its investigations. Americans from various walks of life were targeted, including prominent

In the early 1950s, while McCarthy was becoming an increasingly powerful figure in Washington, he received a medal for his service as a marine during World War II. He is congratulated by Colonel John R. Lanigan.

scientists who spoke out against the use of nuclear weapons. Pacifist groups who were against war also came under suspicion. An example was the Women's International League for Peace and Freedom, founded by the social reformer Jane Addams.

In 1950, Congress passed the Internal Security Act (McCarran Act), requiring groups with ties to the Communist party to register with the government. Anyone suspected of subversion could be finger printed. A Senate Internal Security Subcommittee was set up to work with the FBI.

The Rosenberg Case

That same year (1950) a young married couple, Julius and Ethel Rosenberg, were charged with espionage. They were accused of passing secret information on U.S. atomic research to a Soviet agent. Their controversial trial in March lasted just two weeks. Although the Rosenbergs declared their innocence, the "Red Atom Spies," as they were called in news headlines, were convicted and sentenced to die.

Supporters in America and in Europe maintained that the Rosenbergs had not been proven guilty "beyond a reasonable doubt," as American law required. They said the evidence

Ethel and Julius Rosenberg were convicted of espionage on April 5, 1951, and later sentenced to be executed.

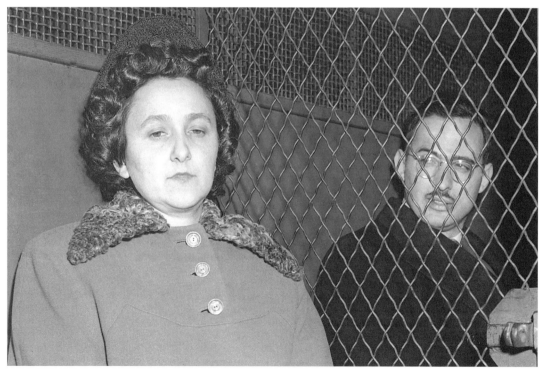

In spring 1951, attorney Arnold Kinoy received an unexpected visit from Arnold Perl, the scriptwriter for a popular television program called *The Big Story*. Perl explained with alarm that he was going to be fired. "Why?" asked Kinoy. "Simple. I've been blacklisted," said Perl. He explained that a supermarket owner in Syracuse, New York, had called up the sponsors of his program and threatened to boycott their products if Perl continued to write for the program.

The man who complained about Perl had been reading *Red Channels: The Report of Communist Influence in Radio and Television*, published in 1950 by a group who called themselves "Counterattack." In this booklet, former FBI agents listed people in the entertainment industry who might have Communist ties. The booklet was meant to keep these people from finding work.

Perl had been listed as a "Communist sympathizer" because he wrote a script that helped raise money for Russians who needed financial help during World War II. He also attended a peace conference at a well-known New York City hotel in 1947.

His producer and sponsor both told him he could not work unless he "cleared himself." This meant Perl would have to appear before HUAC to answer questions. Then he would be asked to give the committee names of the "subversives" he knew in the TV industry. It was a terrible choice. Perl knew that people he named would in turn be blacklisted.

People whose names appeared on these lists suffered in many ways, and so did their families. They were often harassed and lost their jobs. Children were teased and called ugly names, such as "traitor." Some victims were physically attacked or had their homes vandalized. People painted insulting symbols and words on their homes and cars, usually in the color red.

In the end, Perl followed his conscience and refused to cooperate.

---

against the Rosenbergs was flimsy and uncertain. Demonstrators urged that the Rosenbergs' lives be spared. Famous people, including the Pope, wrote letters urging mercy. Despite several legal appeals to higher courts, the Rosenbergs were executed in 1953. The case continues to puzzle historians who have weighed the evidence. Some critics think the penalty was too harsh, even if the Rosenbergs were guilty of spying.

The Korean War

In June 1950, the year the Rosenbergs were accused of espionage, fighting broke out in Korea, an Asian country that borders China. Communist North Koreans invaded non-Communist South Korea, prompting Truman to send aid and U.S. troops. The troops pushed the North Koreans above the thirty-eighth parallel, north latitude—an imaginary line north of the equator.

At a Senate subcommittee meeting, McCarthy examines a Russian gun used by North Koreans.

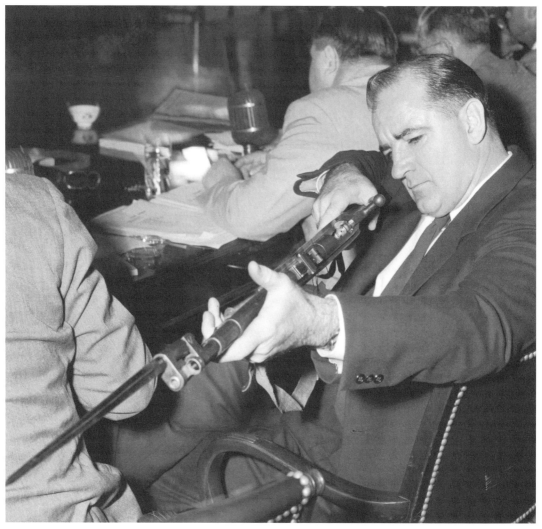

The South Koreans and their allies might have gained control of the country, but Chinese troops arrived to aid the northern forces. This controversial war ended with a compromise in which each side retreated to the thirty-eighth parallel. Critics said the United States should have fought to win the war.

At the Center of the Red Scare

Across America, communism was more and more the main topic of conversation. Several feature films made in the early fifties dealt with the issue. Some contained plots in which loyal Americans came to realize that friends or family members were spies. *Invasion USA* (1952) portrayed a Russian takeover of the United States. Comic strips and magazine stories contained similar plots.

The threat of a Soviet nuclear attack seemed real. Numerous towns built underground bomb shelters, and some citizens built bomb shelters in their yards. Ads for family fallout shelters showed parents and children inside these underground structures, which contained emergency oxygen supplies and sources of water. People discussed which cities the Soviets might strike first if they launched an attack to take over America. Throughout 1950 and 1951, McCarthy was at the center of the growing Red Scare hysteria, warning about the evils of communism at home and abroad. McCarthyism had arrived.

Chapter 4

In June 1951, Joe McCarthy criticized one of the most admired and respected Americans: the former army general George C. Marshall, who was then serving as secretary of defense. In a 600-page speech that focused on Marshall, McCarthy asked, "How can we account for our present situation unless we believe that men high in government are concerting to deliver us to disaster? This must be the product of a great conspiracy, a conspiracy on a scale so immense as to dwarf any previous such venture in the history of men."

Marshall was in poor health and had planned to resign. He did not reply to McCarthy's charges, but many of his friends and supporters did, among them General Dwight D. Eisenhower. A few months after McCarthy's attack, Marshall left Washington.

Next, McCarthy asked that Congress impeach President Truman. Although this proposal didn't win significant support, it seemed that nobody was beyond McCarthy's attacks. Despite his growing power, however, the senator from Wisconsin still held no important committee or leadership positions in Congress. His strength lay in his clever ability to repeatedly make news headlines.

McCarthy did have a visible role at the 1952 Republican convention, which nominated Dwight D. Eisenhower for president and Richard M. Nixon, vice-president. After Eisenhower's victory, however, Republican leaders sought a

President Dwight D. Eisenhower

way to reduce McCarthy's role in the party. The Republicans were finally in power, and it would be embarrassing if McCarthy continued to claim that there were Communists in the government. After McCarthy was named chairman of the Committee on Government Operations, Senate leader Robert Taft told a journalist, "We've got McCarthy where he can't do any harm." The committee handled routine matters, such as property transfers and the assignment of office space. But McCarthy quickly carved out a more important position for himself. He had just been re-elected to the Senate for another six years, and he had some bigger plans of his own.

McCarthy's Subcommittee

McCarthy's committee included a division called the Permanent Subcommittee on Investigations, and he named himself as its head. Instead of pursuing the committee's usual duties, he gave the committee a far broader role in government. At first, McCarthy said he would investigate bribery and corruption. Soon, however, he pledged to continue his fight against Communism. In one interview, he said, "We have complete jurisdiction [authority] in the anti-Communist fight."

McCarthy added conservative senators to his subcommittee and hired a staff. He picked a bright lawyer named Roy Cohn to be the subcommittee's chief counsel (lawyer). Cohn had some experience prosecuting cases against Communists. He urged McCarthy to hire his good friend David Schine to a new, unpaid position called "chief consultant."

In 1953, Roy Cohn became the chief counsel of McCarthy's Permanent Subcommittee on Investigations. He is shown in conference with McCarthy.

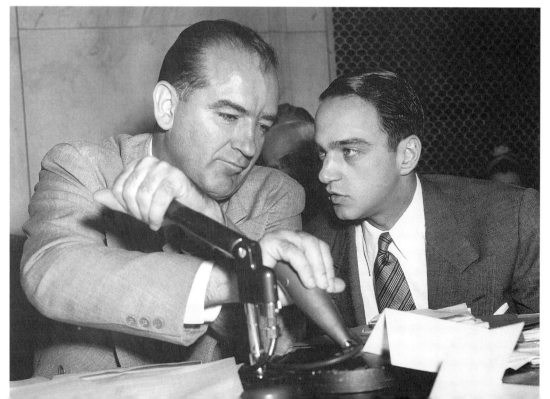

Early in 1953, McCarthy went after the State Department. He charged that department employees could make changes in the files that the department kept on each worker. Employees could therefore eliminate any evidence that might be used against them. McCarthy declared himself ready to help the department root out Communists.

Roy Cohn played a major role on the Permanent Subcommittee, which became known as the "McCarthy Committee." One of its first targets was the Voice of America, which broadcast foreign-language radio programs in about 80 countries. These broadcasts conveyed an American point of view on current events. McCarthy declared there was a subversive plot to sabotage (hurt) the operation, which was run by the State Department.

Once again, McCarthy made headlines. The hearings were on television, but most viewers lacked the information to distinguish truth from fiction. McCarthy did not prove there was sabotage, but he ruined some people's reputations and almost destroyed the Voice of America. One witness committed suicide, even though McCarthy himself later admitted there was no evidence that this man had done anything wrong.

The McCarthy Committee then decided to inspect American-run libraries overseas to ensure they had no books that seemed to support communism. Fearful librarians in Europe removed and burned books that might upset McCarthy, such as the works of the mystery writer Dashiel Hammett, a former member of the Communist party. Some librarians in the United States did the same. Secretary of State John Foster Dulles was told that books by the historian Foster Rhea Dulles had been burned. The secretary of state wondered why his cousin was on the list. President Eisenhower tried to quiet the growing hysteria. In a speech at Dartmouth College that June, he urged Americans, "Don't join the book-burners.... Don't be afraid to go into your library and read every book so long as it does not offend your own ideas of decency."

Although he privately told friends that he hated McCarthy and what he stood for, Eisenhower avoided public confrontations with the senator. He and his aides believed that an open struggle with McCarthy would be undignified and would damage the Republican party. One aide later wrote that Eisenhower must not "get down in the same gutter" with McCarthy. The president hoped that moderate Republicans would confront McCarthy in the Senate.

A Disastrous Association

In April 1953, Roy Cohn and David Schine set out for Europe. The press, often critical, covered their controversial visits to American embassies in Paris, Berlin, Munich, Vienna, Rome, and other cities. In one city, Cohn and Schine said they were investigating "government inefficiency." In others they were hunting for "subversives" or "inspecting books." The pair traveled at government expense, staying at costly hotels. Most Europeans viewed them as arrogant men with no clear authority. Reporters joked about them. In his book, *McCarthy*, Cohn himself later called the trip "a colossal mistake."

Back home, McCarthy was disappointed when the State Department told him to cancel his plans to investigate the Central Intelligence Agency. After this plan collapsed, he fixed his attention on the Government Printing Office, where he found someone in book production who may have once joined the Communist party. McCarthy said his discovery meant that the government's loyalty boards were not properly investigating employees. Next he began investigating private citizens, such as professors who had written books he considered pro-Soviet.

In 1945, physicist Robert Oppenheimer was hailed as the man who led the Manhattan Project, which built the world's first atomic weapons. After these bombs were dropped on Hiroshima and Nagasaki during World War II, Japan surrendered, and the war was over.

Like many of the scientists who worked on the bombs, Oppenheimer was troubled by the massive suffering they caused. He and some of his fellow scientists opposed the development of more destructive atomic weapons and hoped such weapons would never again be used.

After the war, Oppenheimer continued to serve as chairperson of the U.S. Atomic Energy Commission (AEC). The commission was in charge of the government's policy on nuclear weapons. As chairperson, Oppenheimer was routinely investigated and given clearances by military security personnel so that he would have access to top-secret information. In 1953, Oppenheimer was accused of having associated with Communists during the 1930s. His opposition to the new hydrogen bomb (a nuclear bomb that was made by combining hydrogen atoms) also aroused suspicions.

In spring 1954, Oppenheimer endured four weeks of hearings conducted by the AEC, during which he was charged with treason, among other things. U.S. Army General Leslie Groves and the Federation of American Scientists were among his supporters. FBI investigators testified that they had never seen Oppenheimer do anything suspicious during the war. Even so, the AEC declared him a "security risk." He lost his military clearance and was banished from the commission. His reputation was seriously damaged.

For years, Oppenheimer's supporters said he had been unjustly treated. Other scientists urged the government to publicly recognize his achievements and declare his innocence of wrongdoing after years of suspicion. In December 1963, President Lyndon Johnson presented Robert Oppenheimer with the prestigious Fermi Award, given by the Atomic Energy Commission. Noticeably moved, Oppenheimer thanked the president and said his actions showed courage.

Robert Oppenheimer

Rising Criticism

Despite McCarthy's intimidation tactics, which were meant to strike fear in his opponents, more people were speaking out against him. Prominent journalists, including the TV newsman Edward R. Murrow and the author William Shirer, were among those who charged McCarthy with violating people's First Amendment rights. Political cartoonists poked fun at the senator from Wisconsin.

Former beauty queen Jean Kerr married McCarthy on September 29, 1953.

Some journalists called for investigations into McCarthy's misuse of government committees. After the 1952 election, reporters also discovered that he had violated campaign spending laws and had used altered photographs to defeat his political enemy, Millard Tydings of Maryland. McCarthy's assistants took separate newspaper photos of Tydings and of a well-known ex-Communist named Earl Browder, and re-photographed them together so that the two men appeared to be having a conversation.

McCarthy ignored his critics and began a new, large-scale investigation. But first he took time out for his personal life. After a two-week engagement, McCarthy married Jean Kerr, a former college beauty queen who was working in his office as a research assistant. Among their guests were Vice-President and Mrs. Richard Nixon. The 45-year-old senator and his bride spent their three-week honeymoon in the British West Indies. When he returned to Washington, McCarthy was ready to cause another media explosion.

Taking on the Army

Despite his many accusations and investigations, McCarthy had never managed to uncover Communists or spies in the State Department. Now he turned his attention to the U.S. Army. In October, McCarthy declared that he would look into "extremely dangerous espionage" at Fort Monmouth, New Jersey, where the army developed radar and other electronic equipment.

The hearings were conducted at the federal courthouse in New York City. Although they were closed to the public, McCarthy often gave reporters fascinating summaries that kept him and his committee in the news. Dozens of men and women were questioned by McCarthy and Roy Cohn. They asked witnesses offensive questions, such as, "What have you got against this country?"

In the end, the committee did not find evidence of subversive activity at the base. Author Fred J. Cook wrote, "Fort Monmouth, far from producing a flourishing spy ring or a nest of Communists, in the end could not even produce a security risk!" McCarthy was not through with investigating the army, however.

When McCarthy turned his attention to the Republican party, he soon found himself in trouble with the White House. On television, he claimed that there were people in the Republican party who had subversive connections. McCarthy also criticized the party for not taking a strong enough position against Communist China.

President Eisenhower did not comment publicly, but he asked Vice-President Nixon to visit McCarthy. Nixon suggested the senator confine his investigations to Truman's presidency. Eisenhower's staff would handle any problems in his administration. When the press reported that McCarthy had agreed to this suggestion, he denied it. Democrats were pleased by the growing conflict between Eisenhower and McCarthy.

McCarthy's next victim was an army dentist named Irving Peress. When he was drafted in 1952, Peress had declined to answer questions about his political beliefs and associations. His refusal was not uncovered until a year later, when the army reviewed its records in response to Eisenhower's Executive Order 10450. According to the order, federal workers who had "derogatory information" in their files could be dismissed. In the meantime, Peress, who was stationed at Camp Kilmer in New Jersey, had been promoted to major. The army was already in the process of discharging Peress because of his earlier refusal to answer questions, when McCarthy called him before his committee.

Peress appeared, but he refused to answer when McCarthy asked him about any Communist party affiliations or activities.

McCarthy then moved on to personal questions about Peress's family. Peress was deeply upset after this experience and went to his commanding officer to seek an immediate discharge, which was carried out the next day.

The matter did not end there, however. McCarthy had already sent a letter to the secretary of defense insisting that Peress be court-martialed, along with all parties responsible for his promotion and discharge. He ordered Peress to return to the committee, along with the commander of Fort Kilmer, Brigadier General Ralph Zwicker. Zwicker was a distinguished World War II hero with many decorations.

On February 18, 1954, McCarthy personally questioned Zwicker, using tactics that several observers described as unfair and humiliating. The general himself was not responsible for investigating charges against army personnel at Camp Kilmer. Other army officials had authority in these matters. Yet McCarthy continued to badger Zwicker for not acting against Peress, implying that Zwicker ignored the threat of communism at his base. At one point, McCarthy told the general, "You should be removed from any command" and declared that Zwicker was "not fit to wear his uniform."

Chapter 5

THE ARMY—McCARTHY HEARINGS

On March 11, 1954, a middle-aged woman entered a hearing room of the U.S. Senate. Joe McCarthy was waiting to question her. The day before, he had promised the "McCarthy Committee" and the press that something important would happen: He would expose what he called a "Red link" to the U.S. Army.

Annie Lee Moss looked nervous as she arrived. This African-American mother of four had worked at the Pentagon since World War II. The Pentagon suspended her, however, as a result of McCarthy's investigation. Television viewers throughout America saw McCarthy accuse Moss of being a member of the Communist party. He expressed horror that "a known Communist" was working at the Pentagon as a code clerk, who probably had access to top-secret material.

It soon became clear that although Moss ran a machine that transmitted coded messages, she did not know how to decode them. McCarthy urged Moss to "confess" she was a Communist and had paid dues to the Communist party. She emphatically denied these charges.

Another senator, Stuart Symington of Missouri, interrupted McCarthy to ask Moss, "Did you ever hear of Karl Marx?" Moss looked confused and replied, "Who's that?" Muffled laughter could be heard throughout the room as the spectators concluded that the charges against Moss were unfounded.

Further questioning showed that Moss and her family had become poor after she lost her job. Suddenly, McCarthy announced that he had an important appointment and abruptly left the hearing, leaving his lead counsel, Roy Cohn, in charge. Senator Symington told Moss that if the Pentagon did not restore her job, he would help her find another. Then she was excused. The Pentagon did rehire Moss, but the inquiry had upset her deeply.

"Accusation Is Not Proof"

The Moss affair hurt McCarthy, too. Just two days earlier, the television newsman Edward R. Murrow had provided viewers with a harsh look at the senator. He exposed McCarthy during his popular news program, *See It Now*. Murrow used selections from McCarthy's investigations to reveal the unproven charges McCarthy routinely leveled at people. Murrow's audience saw McCarthy giggle nervously, harass and insult people, and contradict himself.

At the end of the program, Murrow commented,

> *…the line between investigating and persecuting is a very fine one and the junior senator from Wisconsin has stepped*

over it repeatedly.... We must not confuse dissent with disloyalty. We must remember always that accusation is not proof and that conviction depends on due process of law.... We cannot defend freedom abroad while deserting it at home.

CBS, Murrow's network, received the largest response to any program it had ever broadcast. More than 90 percent of those who called or wrote letters praised Murrow. He offered McCarthy equal time on his show to reply to his criticism, and McCarthy sent his filmed response to CBS. In his typical fashion, he also contacted the ALCOA company, which sponsored *See It Now*, and threatened to investigate them for backing a subversive broadcast.

Murrow and CBS knew McCarthy might strike back. Murrow told a friend, "Let's face it, McCarthy can't hurt me except economically. I was born with an outside toilet, and I can go out the same way." But Murrow was upset to receive anonymous calls threatening his family.

He aired McCarthy's filmed reply, during which the senator attacked Murrow and implied that he was a Communist sympathizer. After the program was aired, letters and phone calls still favored Murrow over McCarthy. That June, Murrow would receive the Freedom House Award, with this citation: "Free men were heartened by his courage in exposing those who would divide us by exploiting our fears."

The Army vs. McCarthy

All that spring, more trouble brewed for McCarthy. On March 11, the Army issued a 34-page report charging him with seeking favored treatment for his associate, David Schine. That story had begun the previous June, when Schine was drafted. Roy Cohn

McCarthy's reported attempts to gain special treatment for Private David Schine, shown here, led to the Army–McCarthy hearings.

and McCarthy had tried to get Schine commissioned as an officer, but the army refused. Next, they asked Army Secretary Robert Stevens to assign Schine to a post near New York City. That way he could continue working with their committee. Stevens cooperated, and Schine went to Fort Dix, New Jersey, for basic training.

The army report listed 44 incidents in which Cohn or McCarthy pressed army officials to give Schine special treatment. While he was at Fort Dix, Schine spent time on McCarthy committee activities and received more passes to leave the base than any of his peers. The report also said that Cohn had threatened to "wreck the army" and once declared, "This is war!" to get his way with military officials. In light of these charges, the Senate ordered a full inquiry.

McCarthy charged that the army was trying to blackmail him into ending his investigations into military subversion. Joseph Nye Welch, a respected Boston trial lawyer, was to represent the U.S. Army. McCarthy and Cohn said they would represent themselves.

The Army–McCarthy hearings were televised, and millions of Americans watched them. For 14 days, Secretary Stevens presented evidence, interrupted continually by McCarthy. At one point, Stevens said, "I may say that during my tenure as Secretary of the Army, there is no record that matches this persistent, tireless effort to obtain special consideration and privileges for this man." Army witnesses described Cohn's angry outbursts when they did not grant his requests.

When McCarthy himself testified, he introduced as evidence a copy of a letter that was supposedly signed by FBI director J. Edgar Hoover. But Hoover said he had not written it. Welch called the letter "a perfect phony" and tried to get McCarthy to reveal its origins. McCarthy refused. Instead, he changed the subject, raging about communism in the Central Intelligence Agency and at nuclear weapons plants.

The tide was going against McCarthy and Cohn, and disaster loomed. McCarthy had heard that Fred Fisher, a young member of Welch's firm, had once been a member of the Lawyer's Guild. HUAC considered the guild subversive. Fisher and Welch had agreed that he would not work on this case, knowing that McCarthy might use this information against them. As Welch was questioning Cohn one day, McCarthy impatiently broke in to attack Fisher, accusing Welch of bringing a Communist into the case.

The army's lawyer, Joseph N. Welch (sitting, left) looks discouraged after his harsh exchange with McCarthy over Fred Fisher, an attorney at Welch's law firm.

Welch was indignant. He said, "Until this moment, Senator, I think I never really gauged your cruelty or recklessness." Still, McCarthy would not back down, even though Cohn was shaking his head as if to tell McCarthy to stop. Welch finally said, "You've done enough. Have you no sense of decency, sir, at long last? Have you left no sense of decency?"

The Senate Considers Censure

After the hearings ended, people generally agreed that McCarthy and Cohn had been shameful and often disorderly. Joseph Welch was widely praised, and President Eisenhower complimented him privately at the White House before Welch returned home. The investigative committee issued separate reports on August 31. The Democrats' report was more critical of McCarthy and Cohn and focused on instances when they behaved improperly. Most Republicans thought there was not enough evidence to reach a clear conclusion.

Senator Ralph Flanders of Vermont, a Republican, was an exception. He had bravely spoken against McCarthy in the past. Now he asked the Senate to consider a resolution to censure (officially criticize) McCarthy. This was a serious resolution, and to this day, it is rarely introduced in Congress. Censure is less severe than expulsion, but it indicates dishonorable behavior.

A special two-party committee headed by Republican Arthur Watkins of Utah was appointed to consider the matter.

Vermont Senator Ralph Flanders, standing on the right, testifies at the hearing of the committee that considered whether to censure Joseph McCarthy.

While a Senate committee considered whether to censure McCarthy, the Wisconsin senator held a press conference.

The hearings were more quiet than the Army-McCarthy sessions and took less than three weeks. Chairman Watkins maintained order, and McCarthy hired an attorney this time. He continued to attack his critics, calling Watkins "stupid," for example. The group recommended that McCarthy be censured on two counts: his abuse of witnesses (chiefly General Ralph Zwicker) and his disrespectful treatment of senatorial committees.

McCarthy Is Denounced

Two-thirds of the Senate members voted to censure McCarthy. They did not attack his anti-Communist agenda—only his methods of investigation. They criticized McCarthy for not behaving with honor and dignity.

Asked to comment on the vote, McCarthy said, "I wouldn't exactly call it a vote of confidence, but I don't feel I've been lynched." He remained in the Senate and still had his position as committee chairman. His devoted followers continued to support him, and he was invited to speak at meetings of militant anti-Communists.

McCarthy had lost his political power, however, and most of his public support. He was largely ignored when he spoke in the Senate, and reporters showed little interest in him. The White House formally snubbed him by announcing that neither Senator nor Mrs. McCarthy would appear on any future guest lists.

McCarthy's pride was hurt. As a result, he sometimes drank heavily, and his health deteriorated. One bright spot came during his final years, when he and Jean adopted a baby girl. McCarthy told friends that the family planned to live on a cattle ranch in Arizona. But this was not to be. In April 1957, he was admitted to Bethesda Naval Hospital and treated for an inflamed liver. He died on May 2, 1957, at the age of 48.

McCarthy's Legacy

Although the man was gone, the search for Communist subversives did not die. By the mid-fifties, there was a complex system of security boards in place to check the "loyalty" of people employed in government or in government-related jobs. Almost 10 million Americans went through a clearance process during the fifties. Such investigations went on in secret, and people who were considered disloyal often kept the matter quiet instead of fighting publicly to defend themselves.

HUAC continued investigating people whom it considered a threat to America. Some members of the committee attacked immigrants from Eastern Europe, Asia, and Latin America. Over the years, politicians used congressional power to investigate labor unions, liberal organizations, and groups that advocated civil rights for minorities.

Eventually, the Supreme Court struck down some of the programs and laws that were passed during the McCarthy years. The court ruled that the government's programs to determine employee loyalty were unconstitutional. It declared that people accused of disloyalty should have access to files about themselves. During the 1960s, the court struck down parts of repressive laws passed in the 1950s. For many victims of McCarthyism, however, the Supreme Court decisions came too late. Some men and women were unable to restore their damaged reputations or rebuild their lives.

In the years since McCarthyism gripped the nation, thoughtful Americans have tried to understand why the nation allowed a political extremist to gain so much power. The troubling era that was named for the Wisconsin senator serves as a reminder that people's rights can be trampled whenever fear overcomes good judgement, and when accusations and distortions replace due process of law. Even in "the land of the free," freedom cannot be taken for granted.

Chronology

The Life of Joseph McCarthy

November 14, 1908	Joseph McCarthy born in Grand Chute, Wisconsin.
1922	Finishes grammar school and builds successful chicken farm.
1928	Enrolls in high school and receives diploma in one year.
1935	Receives law degree from Marquette University, in Wisconsin.
1939	Elected circuit court judge.
June 1942– December 1944	Serves in U.S. Marine Corps during World War II.
1946	Elected to U.S. Senate from Wisconsin.
February 1950	Makes news headlines after charging that Communist subversives are working in U.S. State Department.
1950–53	Accuses numerous public officials of Communist activities.
1952	Re-elected to U.S. Senate. Marries Jean Kerr.
1953	As chairman of Senate Subcommittee on Investigations, probes alleged Communist activities.
1954	Claims U.S. Army ignored Communist subversives. Army counters with charges that McCarthy used improper tactics to gain favors for former committee member, David Schine. Army–McCarthy hearings receive nationwide radio and television coverage. McCarthy is censured in Senate.
May 2, 1957	Dies in Bethesda, Maryland.

The Life of the Nation

1919	Congress creates Anti-Radical Division to investigate and prosecute persons who may threaten U.S. government.

1919–1920	Hundreds of Russian immigrants are deported for political reasons.
October 1929	Stock market crashes; Great Depression brings years of massive poverty and sparks intense political debates.
1932	Franklin D. Roosevelt elected President; launches New Deal programs to ease Depression.
1938	Congress passes Hatch Act, which bans Communist party members from holding federal jobs.
	Congress establishes House Un-American Activities Committee (HUAC) to investigate Communist subversives.
1945	Truman becomes president upon death of Roosevelt.
1947	Truman Doctrine outlines policy of containment of Communism.
	Executive Order 9835 authorizes large-scale probes into loyalty of federal employees.
October 1947	HUAC begins probing subversion in film industry.
1948	Harry S. Truman wins a new term as president.
1948–49	Soviets impose blockade on Berlin, Germany.
1949	Communists win revolutionary war in China, driving Nationalists out of mainland.
	Soviet Union tests nuclear weapons.
	United States and western allies found NATO.
January 1950	Former government official Alger Hiss is convicted of perjury after denying under oath that he was a Russian spy.
1950	Congress passes Internal Security Act (McCarran Act), which requires Communist-linked groups to register with government.
1950–1953	Korean War ends with creation of Communist North Korea and non-Communist South Korea.
1952	Republican Dwight Eisenhower elected president.
1953	Executive Order 10450 states that federal workers who have "derogatory information" in their files can be dismissed.
	Death of Soviet leader Joseph Stalin eases Cold War tensions.
	Julius and Ethel Rosenberg are executed after being convicted in controversial espionage case.

Glossary

affiliation Connection with individuals or a group.

blacklist A list of people who are punished or boycotted, often by refusing to hire them.

Bolsheviks Members of a radical political party in Russia that sparked a revolution to replace Czarist rule with communism.

communism A political and economic system in which the government owns all business and property, and the profits are shared by all.

contempt (as in "to hold in contempt") To ignore or disrespect the authority of a court of law.

due process of law Legal procedures that provide for the rights of defendants.

Eastern or Soviet bloc A group of nations in eastern and central Europe that came under Soviet domination after World War II.

interrogate To question someone, usually in an official capacity.

libel A statement about a person that unfairly creates a negative impression of him or her.

loyalty oath A statement in which a person swears to be faithful to his or her government or to some organization.

McCarthyism The use of personal tactics and highly publicized, undocumented claims to oppose someone suspected of subversive behavior or beliefs.

prosecute To carry out a legal action in a court of law against someone accused of a crime.

sabotage To willfully damage or destroy.

subversion Acts meant to overthrow or destroy the government.

subversives People who commit subversive acts.

Source Notes

Chapter One

Page 5: "Have you ever been a member..." and "I would prefer..." Victor Navasky. *Naming Names.* New York: Viking, 1980, p. viii.

Page 5: "Don't present me with the choice...to be an informer." Ibid., p. ix.

Page 10: "They remember him..." David M. Oshinsky. *A Conspiracy So Immense.* New York: The Free Press, 1983, p. 4.

Page 13: "take possession of our American Government..." Robert P. Ingalls. *Point of Order: A Profile of Senator Joe McCarthy.* New York: G.P. Putnam's Sons, 1981, p. 29.

Page 14: "We have never graduated..." Richard H. Rovere. *Senator Joe McCarthy.* Cleveland: World Publishing Company, 1959, p. 84.

Page 14: "His pile-driving lefts and rights..." Oshinsky, p. 13.

Page 17: "I've always felt..." Ibid., p. 16.

Page 18: "consciousness of the art and economics." T.H. Watkins. *The Great Depression: America in the 1930s.* Boston: Little Brown, 1993, p. 251.

Page 19: "to investigate, humiliate, meddle with anything..." Michael Dorman. *Witch Hunt.* New York: Delacorte, 1976, p. 19.

Chapter Two

Page 21: "my 73-year-old opponent." Ingalls, p. 18.

Page 21: "Judge McCarthy, whose burning ambition..." Rovere, p. 93.

Page 24: "Everyone knows that..." Jack Anderson and Ronald W. May. *McCarthy: The Man, the Senator, the 'Ism.'* Boston: The Beacon Press, 1952, p. 111.

Page 27: "free peoples who are resisting..." Richard M. Freeland. *The Truman Doctrine and the Origins of McCarthyism.* New York: Knopf, 1971, pp. 85–86.

Page 28: "For a week, this committee..." Dorman, p. 69.

Page 31: "a mighty offensive…" and "in which free institutions can exist." Mabel E. Casner and Ralph H. Gabriel, et al. *Story of the American Nation.* New York: Harcourt Brace & World, Inc., 1962, p. 653.

Chapter Three

Page 37: "Check before you sign…" Michael Barson. *Better Red Than Dead.* New York: Hyperion, 1992, unpaginated.

Page 37: "That's it…" Rovere, p. 123.

Page 37: "engaged in a showdown fight" that pitted "our Western Christian world" against "the atheistic Communist world." Ingalls, p. 42.

Page 38: "those who have been treated so well…" Ibid., p. 42.

Page 39: "I will be glad to give him the names of those 57 card-carrying Communists." Dorman, p. 145.

Page 40: "I want him to name…" Ibid., p. 149.

Page 41: "thinks this should be…" Ibid., p. 151.

Page 41: "It's just one of those tasks…" Barson, unpaginated.

Page 41: "one of the most complete investigations…" Dorman, p. 153.

Page 43: "utterly false" and "seriously jeopardized, if not destroyed." Ibid., pp. 154–155.

Page 43: "loud-mouthed and irresponsible." Oshinsky, p. 122.

Page 44: "I will stand or fall on this one…" Burt Hirschfeld. *Freedom in Jeopardy: The Story of the McCarthy Years.* New York: Julian Messner, 1969, p. 57.

Page 44: "a fraud and a hoax" and "half-truths and untruth." Ingalls, p. 60.

Page 44: "delighted his whole case…" Hirschfeld, p. 60.

Page 44: "A signal to the traitors…" Ingalls, p. 60.

Page 47: "Why?…. Simple, I've been blacklisted." Arthur Kinoy. *Rights on Trial.* Cambridge, MA: Harvard University Press, 1983, p. 94.

Chapter Four

Page 50: "How can we account…" Ingalls, p. 68.

Page 51: "We've got McCarthy…" Rovere, p. 188.

Page 52: "We have complete jurisdiction…" Ingalls, p. 92.

Page 53: "Don't join the book-burners…." Dorman, p. 195.

Page 54: "a colossal mistake." Oshinsky, p. 81.

Page 54: "get down in the same gutter." Ibid., p. 351.

Page 57: "What have you got against…" Ibid., p. 339.

Page 58: "Fort Monmouth, far from producing…" Fred J. Cook. *The Nightmare Decade: The Life and Times of Joseph R. McCarthy.* New York: Random House, 1971, p. 456.

Page 59: "You should be removed…" Dorman, p. 212.

Chapter Five

Page 61: "Did you ever hear of Karl Marx?" and "Who's that?" Dorman, p. 3.

Page 61: "the line between investigating…" Joseph E. Persico. *Edward R. Murrow.* New York: McGraw-Hill, 1988, p. 378.

Page 62: "Let's face it…" Ibid., p. 381.

Page 62: "Free men were heartened…" Ibid., p. 394.

Page 64: "wreck the Army" Ingalls, p. 113.

Page 64: "This is war!" Ibid., p. 125.

Page 64: "I may say that during my tenure…" Ibid., p. 118.

Page 65: "Until this moment, Senator…" Oshinsky, p. 462.

Page 65: "You've done enough…." Ingalls, p. 129.

Page 68: "I wouldn't exactly call it…" Rovere, p. 231.

Further Reading

Black, Wallace B. and Blashfield, Jean F. *Hiroshima and the Atomic Bomb* (World War II 50th Anniversary series). Glendale, CA: Crestwood House, 1993.

Cross, Robin. *Aftermath of War* (World War II series). New York: Thomson Learning, 1994.

Devaney, John. *America Goes to War: 1941* (World War II series). New York: Walker & Co., 1991.

Duden, Jane. *1950s* (Timelines series). Glendale, CA: Crestwood House, 1990.

Epler, Doris M. *The Berlin Wall: How It Rose and Why It Fell*. Brookfield, CT: The Millbrook Press, 1992.

Kallen, Stuart A. *The Stalin Era (Rise and Fall of the Soviet Union)*. Minneapolis, MN: Abdo & Daughters, 1992.

Kort, Michael G. *The Cold War*. Brookfield, CT: The Millbrook Press, 1993.

_____. *China Under Communism*. Brookfield, CT: The Millbrook Press, 1993.

Steins, Richard. *The Allies Against the Axis: World War II*. New York: Twenty-First Century Books, 1994.

_____. *The Postwar Years: The Cold War and Atomic Age (1950-59)*. New York: Twenty-First Century Books, 1994.

Warren, James A. *Cold War: The American Crusade Against the Soviet Union and World Communism, 1945–1990*. New York: Lothrop, Lee & Shephard, 1996.

Web Sites

For more information on Joseph McCarthy, including quotes and links to other Web sites, go to:
http://www.sirius.com/~mcjester/writings/joemccarthy.html

To hear selections of McCarthy's speeches, go to:
http://www.webcorp.com/mccarthy/mccarthypage.htm

To read about the Hollywood Blacklist, go to:
http://www.english.upenn.edu/~afilreis/50s/blacklist.html

For a Nuclear Age Timeline, pre-1940's through 1990's, go to:
http://www.em.doe.gov/timeline

For more information on the House Un-American Activities Committee and censorship, go to:
http://www.moderntimes.com/palace/huac.htm

For photographs, essays, and archives on the Berlin Wall, go to:
http://www.appropriatesoftware.com/Berlin Wall

Index

Photo Credits

Cover and pages 4, 12, 23, 25, 29, 33, 39, 43, 45–46, 48, 52, 55–56, 63, 65, and 67: ©UPI/Corbis-Bettmann; pages 7, 22, and 32: courtesy of the National Archives; pages 9 and 66: ©Corbis-Bettmann; page 15: courtesy of the Herbert Hoover Presidential Library-Museum; pages 18 and 51: ©Blackbirch Press, Inc.; page 27: courtesy of The Library of Congress.